a map to mercy

a map to mercy

elizabeth jarrett andrew

WINNER OF THE ORISON CHAPBOOK PRIZE

A Map to Mercy

Print ISBN: 978-1-949039-66-5
E-book ISBN: 978-1-949039-67-2

Orison Books
PO Box 8385
Asheville, NC 28814
www.orisonbooks.com

Cover design by Luke Hankins and Addison Skigen.

Manufactured in the U.S.A.

ORISON
BOOKS

CONTENTS

I HAVE CANCER. On a hospital bed, I lean shoulder-to-shoulder, backs against the wall, with a white-coated oncologist. His large Mediterranean nose reminds me of my uncle's. *Your illness is terminal*, he confirms. In the face of death his presence comforts me. I relax into his shoulder, into the wall, even further back, falling into a sweet, encompassing silence.

*

FOR WEEKS AFTER I dreamt this moment, the silence was so near all I needed was a walk in the woods or ten minutes on my knees to be saturated again. Quiet mind, beating body. Welcome dissolution. Rest unlike any I'd known. Freedom. Peace. Tender, vibrating presence. Communion, union. True self in the form of love. The close, swelling emptiness I called God.

Silence pulsed through my being. In the dream I'd accepted an invitation: *You can rest; you will be held.* I no longer needed to believe this because I *knew*. I knew even while I was awake, going to work, cleaning the house, playing with my daughter.

Then time passed. The feeling dissipated, and my busy mind returned. What if the dream was prescient and I really *was* dying of cancer? Shouldn't I do something? Prayer again became the usual scrambling only now layered with grief at losing that merciful silence. For twenty-plus years I'd meditated, which generally meant floundering through fields of swirling thoughts, clutching my breath like a guide rope, desperately wanting help from my Christian tradition and finding little, certainly never finding rest. Now, with the dream dormant in my bones, the posturing clergy, credal pronouncements, and relentless *busy-ness* of Sunday morning worship grew intolerable. Noise bombarded every second of the service. I returned home so snippy from seeing the theatrics of my mind enacted on stage, my wife insisted I quit. Instead I amped up the meditation, because how else might I find again that blessed quiet?

But I could not recreate what I'd tasted as grace.

Somehow—a series of coincidences, a comment from a friend leading to a podcast recommending a book I'd read two decades earlier but was now ready to ingest—I found Centering Prayer, a contemporary rendition of an ancient monastic practice from the Egyptian desert. I drank it like a thirsty pilgrim. Unlike my floundering Buddhist meditation, and contrary to everything I'd encountered in my milquetoast United Methodist tradition, Centering Prayer embraced both the fullness *and* emptiness of spiritual experience, what Christians call the *via positiva* and the *via negativa*. I'd experienced both in my dream: the warm shoulder of my oncologist, whose whispered voice tenderly named the truth—and utter dissolution. Centering Prayer immersed me in a divine pervasive presence which feels like absence; it ushered me into my own essential absence which seems like a presence. It unfurled before me a path back to that pulsing, trustworthy peace in the face of death.

*

TODAY WHEN I kneel before my candle, I finish pleas for humanity's release from suffering, for our threatened environment, for our broken democracy; I unburden myself of my longings because this is what prayer has been for me from the start, my mother beside me in bed, coaxing—"Dear God"—and still is, reflexively; I wouldn't know what to do with my ache otherwise. Then I recite my intention: "I consent to Your presence and movement within me." I begin Centering Prayer. As soon as I notice my thoughts, I use a sacred word to return to my intention. *Mercy.* A sacred word is like a bone you throw to your enthusiastic mind. You're to rest in open-hearted stillness, which I don't ever; I just think and throw bones. The teachers say this is enough. I try to believe them.

*

MERCY IS NOT the word I would have chosen. Heck, the last thing I wanted during prayer was another word, however sacred. I was seeking silence. Centering Prayer's definition of a "word" is wide, fortunately—an image will do, or the breath—so initially I fell back on years of meditation and focused on breath. The reliable in-rush of air, the still turning point, the deflation. Breath as a blanket of warmth. Breath as a flush of movement. Sure, I was as distracted as ever, but at least I was full of breath! My prayer was jammed with concentrated, enthusiastic love of breathing.

And I was doing it wrong. Various forms of meditation exercise different spiritual muscles; concentrative forms build focus, and Centering Prayer, I quickly learned, strengthens willingness. The prayer works with intention and release. Once breath reminded me of my purpose, I should let it go.

A year into the practice I was kneeling before my candle when a memory from the massage table returned: my body worker pressing a sore spot beneath my right shoulder blade. It hurt. I focused my attention there, narrowing my awareness down to that muscle's ache. This took effort. My energy was directed. She noticed, and suggested instead that I simply be aware. Then I sensed the hurt in a broader arena of radiating warmth; I felt the ebb and flow of breath and my breasts pressed into the table and my diffuse, circulating energy. Awareness is consciousness that is open, relaxed, receptive, unattached. The difference between attention and awareness, I saw, is the difference between letting go and letting be. Attention, even to breath, is an exercise of the ego, and Centering Prayer endeavors to relax the ego's grip. Every one of the countless times I consent to the source of life within and beyond me, signaled by my sacred word, I make an internal bow. *Not me, not my thoughts, but You.*

Oh. In the first of hundreds, thousands, of releases, I let my breath be. And conceded. For the sake of that exquisite silence I would take on a word.

*

MERCY FOUND ME. I struck the match, knelt, and *mercy* in neon flashed in my mind. I didn't like it, so I tried *love* and *open*, both of which seemed gratuitous; I tried *Spirit*, which just felt silly. I tried *Yahweh* and it was perfect, the open *Yah* on the inhale, the surrendering *weh* on the exhale, the beautiful cycle of the nameless name of God washing me inside and out. I learned that *Allah* also weds God and breath. Both names resonate with the essence of creation, an unsayable Mystery.

Neither was my word. Every time I knelt, *mercy* whispered in my ear and I reacted: What kind of antiquated patriarchal God-speak was this, rearing up from the recesses of my subconscious? A friend called mercy watered down compassion, and I agreed. To have mercy, one party condescends to another, presuming judgment only to erase it. Or worse: "For God has consigned men to disobedience, that He may have mercy upon all," the apostle

Paul wrote, making humans the intentional victims of God's narcissistic plan and inflicting generations with debilitating shame. Not to mention excluding women. I threw an internal tantrum: The brunt of hierarchical violence has been born mostly by women and dark skinned people and the poor; the whole sin and salvation tradeoff has done nothing but damage our planet, and as a mother I knew no loving parent would create beautiful humanity only to have them grovel at Her feet. Mercy seemed a sorry remnant of a theology I'd discarded decades ago.

I had the sensation of wrestling with an angel, or maybe with my sister, bending her arm back until she cried, "Mercy!" Her name is Marcy. *Mmrrssee*: the sounds are deep in my psyche, and beloved. What if my sacred word was just a string of sounds? All I needed was a signal of my intention. Father Thomas Keating, progenitor of Centering Prayer, tells a story about an old deaf monk who misheard the instructions and for months happily used "Cheerios!" as his sacred word. *Mmrrssee* would suffice.

*

WHEN THE DEVIL tempted Jesus in the desert, Jesus retorted with scripture: "Man shall not live by bread alone but by every word that proceeds from the mouth of God." Early Christian monastics understood the mind to be our desert, the myriad distractions our devil. Give the devil a sacred phrase as Jesus did, they taught, and turn away. The phrase chosen by those wise north African Abbas and Immas became the Jesus Prayer: "Lord Jesus Christ, son of God, have mercy on me, a sinner." This simple practice—note the internal distraction, then use holy words to return to your intention—was preserved behind monastery walls and in Eastern

Orthodoxy for seventeen centuries. It broke into modern, Western consciousness only recently, thanks especially to Thomas Keating, in the form of Centering Prayer.

My practice was well established, *mmrrsee* wearing grooves into my brain, when I learned this history—and panicked all over again. What if the Jesus Prayer and its contemporary offspring, Centering Prayer, were some creepy Christian indoctrination? What if in its form or substance it perpetuated a cosmology that denigrated my body and being? *Lord,* patriarchal and monarchical, I outright rejected as a preface to Jesus's name—as did Jesus himself. *Jesus* I was taught to adore as a storybook character and emulate as a social activist but never actually worship. Evangelicals and the secular Americans they've persuaded find this unfathomable, but liberal Christians prefer to worship abstractions. I could honor *Christ*, that exquisite union between divinity and creation, but Jesus himself made me squirm. *On me* made me lowly, cowering at mercy's beneficence. The traditional tail of the prayer, *a sinner*, I chopped off.

Daughter of Eve, royally screwed from the start, the good God leaning against a tree in the Garden intoning, "I told you so"… Nope. I couldn't stomach it.

The trouble was, I also found this history compelling. Millenia of church teaching, especially in the east, lifts up the Jesus Prayer as Christianity's most powerful. I imagined thousands of faithful throughout time wearing grooves into those simple words, trusting them with their weight, propelled by them into lives of devotion. What if *mercy* had risen from an archetypal origin in my psyche? When I traveled with my father back to the tiny Albanian Italian village of his ancestors, the local priest—tall, gregarious, bubbly, with a large nose—welcomed us into the parish hall to dig through church records. Walking down the corridor we passed a small room where a woman sat in adoration before a candle and what I later learned was the Eucharist. The priest explained that the town rotated through so that, twenty-four hours a day, 365 days a year, someone was praying. My father found this absurd. I wept with wonder.

Deep in my impulse toward silence was this heritage. I'm not alone. I belong to a lineage of Christians tracing back to the Good Teacher Himself who met God in both silence and crowds. I might not like the word *mercy*, I might despise the theology surrounding it, but like much of scripture and institutional religion and Sunday morning's rush to get out of the house and, damn it, worship committee debates about which is better, bread or wafers, this tradition was mine.

*

EVEN NOW, WRITING this, I blush to admit that my prayer word is *mercy*. It reflects poorly on me. I'm unenlightened, caught up in bad doctrine, a fraud of a feminist, a failure of a twenty-first century liberal. I'd rather you didn't know. Here, in another of thousands of consents, I take my discomfort and sit with it. This struggle with mercy is really about what gets in the way of surrender. I wrestle with the word on my way to—for the sake of—that prized silence.

*

SILENCE IS A cloud surrounding my body. When I breathe in, the cloud contracts. When I breathe out, the cloud expands. The refrigerator purrs, I wonder about lunch, in seconds I'm careening down the highway of miscellany—my usual speed, the usual road—until I realize what's happened and screech to a halt. Did I choose this digression? Or am I a victim of it? How much of my daily rushing after this or that is similar, a frantic ride out of town that seems like freedom but lands me nowhere, out of gas? I resist the label "sinner" but "distractible" sure fits, as does "needy" and "undisciplined" and "helpless." I can't stop myself from jumping in that red convertible and hitting the pedal.

But now I've noticed. In prayer I see my habitual grasping after significance, existence, anything, and know this to be the least of my flaws. At dinner my ten-year-old is dysregulated; to get her to eat we must remind her to take every bite, and it's exhausting—I snap. November descends ominously on Minnesota, making me irritable. I prep an awesome class, then bungle it. Grief at the racial injustices of our city makes me rage at my partner because she's an easier target. Newspaper headlines boil my blood, as they should, but on a dime I turn cynical or bitter. In years past I've beat myself up for such things but lately that seems a waste of time. "Guilt feelings that last longer than half a minute are neurotic," Thomas Keating taught, an insight born either of unconscionable irresponsibility or sober assurance. A professor of Black American literature once told me, in a similar vein, that white guilt is unproductive. What matters is responsibility.

At some point in my forties, either due to age or prayer, my sense of self finally solidified enough to no longer feel threatened by its fundamental brokenness. I'm a mess, and really, that's okay. Creation's forward motion takes precedence over my unworthiness. Better to accept my shortcomings, those fleeting and those festering at the root, and move on.

This is the exercise of Centering Prayer. I am an addict, addicted to the self, admitting just how unmanageable my life has become. When I cry *mercy*, I say, "You small self, trying so desperately to matter: Have mercy on me. Let me go." First *I* must show mercy on me. Only then might I accept a compassion wider than my own.

I breathe. I turn my heart, if only for a microsecond, toward the stillness vibrating between my body and the city's sounds. All my relentless thoughts present the perfect opportunity to choose, again and again. I choose quiet. I choose patience and deliberation and receptivity. I choose life.

*

"FOR GOD HAS consigned all men to disobedience, that he may have mercy upon all." Surely these words are stained past recognition, by culture and history and translation; surely Paul meant "The universe created us with rampant imperfections because that way we long for wholeness. Besides—only brokenness leaves space for fierce, binding love to connect us, one to another." Actually, whether or not Paul meant this doesn't matter much to me, because this is how the world works.

*

MERCY, I REPEAT. This word I never use otherwise is the bell I silently ring to return to my intention. *Mercy* means *show forbearance upon my offenses. Mercy* means *bless me with your favor. Mercy* means *erase whatever in me gets in the way of Life.* Thoughts spiral off—another friend with cancer, a toothache, the pile of laundry—until I wake up: Remember your intention? For now, for twenty minutes, you're submitting to a love bigger than you can manage. *Mercy.* For the beat of a breath, I wait.

The word evolved through medieval Latin's *merced*, meaning a price paid or wages. If I want quiet, if I want union, the price I pay is my noisy separate self. Over and over. I also want to be somebody, and I pay this want in wages. My cancer dream was prescient after all, warning me of the ego-death I must endure on the way to silence.

Then there's the Greek, which, oddly, I sang growing up in our small Methodist choir of four because our brilliant organist was classically trained: *Christe eleison*, Christ have mercy, our boys' choir voices arching through the white-walled sanctuary. And from the pulpit, Daniel: *Give ear, O God, and hear; open Your eyes… We do not make requests of you because we are righteous, but because of your great mercy.* The plea for mercy comes first from my people, a ragtag, barely integrated, dying congregation of believers caught in an flawed institution, loving one another and trying our darnedest to be good. *Save us from what separates us from You. Return us to what matters.*

Only today do I grasp what we were saying.

*

MY FAMILY SOMETIMES prays with a group of Native women down at the Mississippi River. Water is life, so we plant our feet in the sand and offer thanks. One morning, the Ojibwe elder Sharon Day translated her prayer for us: "Most kind creator, Gizhay Manitou, have pity on us." *Pity* landed a familiar gut-punch. "All of creation existed without us," she said, "and will exist after us." At her feet was a quilt, a copper bowl of river water, a shell cupping burnt sage. Behind her the river eddied and flowed. "We are dependent on creation. We're dependent on the web of life. It is not dependent on us." We are mighty, yes, but also small and helpless, and remembering this is good.

That I heard this truth more clearly from a tradition other than my own was an irony not lost on me.

My dislike of mercy, my unwillingness to show mercy toward myself—these are dams I've erected around my heart, cutting myself off from mercy's river. When I breathe in, silence pours through me. When I breathe out, I am a great lung of quiet. I turn away from my flurry of thoughts, only for now, only for twenty minutes, using the word and the tradition I've been given. When the bell rings I'll obsess again, I'll make the peanut butter and jelly sandwiches, I'll make love, I'll be my messy ordinary selfish self. For now, in the small sphere of my being, I practice mercy.

*

TRUTH BE TOLD, some days I *want* to bow down before an almighty God. I want to press my forehead into the dirt. I want a powerful, overpowering divinity because at least that God would be present, unlike the infused hidden energy who inhabits me as much as anyplace else. The divinity I know travels up my spine and asks that I hold my head high—wear my crown—even though some days it's such a burden. I want to lay those heavy jewels aside, place my palms on the ground, and worship something outside of me. Call me un-American, anti-intellectual, masochistic, even, but it's true. I want to submit.

Mercy won't have it. *Mercy* helps me bow, it touches forehead to earth, but then there's nothing, only silence moving like weighty, dark planets. No *deus ex machina.* No booming voice. Definitely no Savior. Just emptiness asking for trust and awareness, asking to move in me, no—not even asking. This prayer is humbler than any bowing down. This prayer is emptiness being emptiness.

*

FOR CENTERING PRAYER to do its work, the teachers recommend two twenty-minute sits daily. One I squeeze in at the beginning of my day but the second's nigh impossible; my daughter's home early from school, ravenous, crashing her body into mine, and one thing cascades into the next until bedtime, when I'm so exhausted I stumble into walls. A solution bubbles up from who-knows-where: Use the Jesus Prayer. Which is how I find myself walking to school one afternoon repeating that ancient Christian mantra that not a year prior I scorned. *Jesus Christ, have mercy on me. Jesus Christ, have mercy on me.* I thumb Tibetan prayer beads in my pocket for a nice interfaith twist. My sneakers lend each step a bounce. Wet autumn leaves plaster the sidewalk.

When my parents baptized me United Methodist, they intended for me a conventional social nicety with moral roots. Not *this.* This is irrational, primitive, so scarily Christian even most Catholics don't pray this way. I cross 28th Street and duck under the low branch of a birch.

What's come over me? Why can't I put my quest for silence aside and just enjoy the walk? Instead I foist words into my consciousness where none are necessary; I squelch my usual reflective meandering in favor of questionable doctrine packaged in magical thinking. This is not me. How have I come to deliberately undermine my best instincts?

It's as though *mercy*, once excavated from some dormant gene, has elbowed out space for its entire unwelcome family. There's nothing, *nothing*, about this prayer I like, except the secret impulse that brings it to my heart. A stirring. A refuge. The school crossing guards hold out their orange flags. Parents converge from every direction. I'm quite sure no one else is fingering prayer beads in their pockets—certainly not the other queer moms and tattooed thirtysomethings; perhaps the Somali dads? Are there Sufis in my midst? In the confounded ways of the Spirit, some core of trustworthiness remains tucked in the pockets of my being while on the surface I'm a freak.

*

TEN THOUSAND CONSENTS. Surrender, passivity, submission, begging for mercy—in the material world these are assaults on dignity. Anathemas. I refuse to bow to anyone, nor to any government, nor to any religion. I have in the past; I've kowtowed to the power of What Others Think, constricting my choice of clothes or work or writing topics to the detriment of my breathing. I have groveled before publishers, with ugly consequences. For years I surrendered to church, in part out of habit but mostly because I believe Christ's body is communal and I thought church the best means of participating. I submitted to church in all its enduring friendships and relentless boredom and stupid dogma and moments of grace, despite the slow languishing of my soul.

Gradually I wake up to these false idols. I will not compromise my agency, my participation in creation, my inner knowing. I will not compromise my spirit.

But I'll kiss the earth. I'll submit to love—I do it daily in my marriage, eating the dairy-free, gluten-free concoctions Emily makes for dinner, admitting my wrongs, caring for her through her bouts with cancer, agreeing to fewer bookshelves because that's not her idea of interior decorating. I do it daily in motherhood, consenting to the obliteration of my focus because Gwyn has the flu, compromising my need for cleanliness in favor of her paper doll enthusiasm, and when she wakes at 6 a.m., interrupting my quiet, I release my disappointment and open my arms to her body, still bed-warm and smelling of sleep. I do it in writing, today even, tackling a subject certain to garner dismissal but which nonetheless presents itself. I surrender in moments when injustice gains such prominence I've no choice but to set aside any plans to trek to the capitol for another protest. I bow shamelessly before these lifegiving forces.

And while I get confused about it, endlessly confused, love—that searing silence which is love—is my God. Prayer is how I remember. *Mercy* is how I bow down.

*

WHAT FRIGHTENS ME most about repeating the Jesus Prayer is how it cancels my usual consciousness. Regardless of what the words mean, this prayer asks that I forsake my thoughts in favor of a formula. Like brainwashing. Silence I can handle—at least silence signals rest—but not this. In the face of obliteration, suddenly I cherish my thoughts. I have great ideas, inspired even. When else will I think them if not while doing dishes or cleaning the litter box? My incessant, internal voice is a gift. No, it's more than that: It's who I am.

At least that's what I assume. Richard Rohr, Franciscan teacher, posits that 90% of our thinking is obsessive, so I test his claim.

On an ordinary ten-minute walk to school, what fills my mind? Images of cabled Irish sweaters from the catalogue in the bathroom. Spinning concerns about Gwyn's attention deficit. I try to think productively, to create a new writing prompt for my students, but instead plan the order in which I'll cook dinner: first get the water boiling, then chop the onions. Richard's right. Most of what happens in my head is schlock. My mind, undirected, is reactive, petty, fearful, repetitive, spinning silly future scenarios of what I'll wear or how I'll lose weight.

Or Richard is wrong—he's underestimated our smallness. "Why are you unhappy?" Wei Wu Wei asks. "Because 99.9 percent of everything you think and of everything you do, is for yourself—and there isn't one." While Christian mystics claim the discursive self is false rather than illusory, the point holds. Not only are my thoughts small; their content is misdirected. In our ordinary thinking, we're trapped. Realizing this is unbearable.

The teachers say there's no cause for concern. While contemplative practice seems to lull the mind into dull blankness, in fact it sharpens reason, intuition, and ingenuity. Centering prayer, the Jesus Prayer, most meditation practices—these reduce the time we chase after thoughts; they stop us from believing our own spinning stories. They crack open the possibility of something more.

On a typical walk to school, I'm a victim, yanked haplessly hither and yon by random thoughts. Consider, by contrast, teaching, after I've given a prompt and half the class taps their pens and looks at the ceiling or gets up to pee and I'm deluged with self-doubt. I could concede to my fear and cut the exercise short, but I don't, I agree to the discomfort because this is what writing feels like; I allow the rustling, pen-scratching silence to be what it is. That I have this choice is a freedom. Or consider my own morning of writing, when I deliberately tame, harness, and ride thoughts. The quiet concentration at my desk, the directed exploration, the prolonged immersion in a story or idea… Writing is a generative engagement not just of my thoughts but of my entire being, and becomes more so when I deliberately choose it by turning off my computer's internet connection and the ringer on my phone. Afterward, in the tradition of Minneapolis native Brenda Ueland, I walk, having postmarked my project and sent it to the subconscious; I moodle, as she called it, mind adrift. That's when ideas come. This, too, is a choice.

What will I give myself to, deliberately and with intention? This increasing capacity to bow down, to choose, springs from Centering Prayer. Whenever my mind isn't required for a specific task, I practice. Thought after stupid thought catches me unaware. I become aware, and then have a choice where none existed prior. I can chase after this relentless interior dialogue because it's *me*, or I can consent to relinquish *me* in favor of something else—silence, nothingness, prayer, presence. The soapy dishwater warming my hands. The smooth curve of a bowl. The counter pressing my hips. These, I'm coming to see, are my liberation.

*

I OUGHT TO know better than to call my thoughts stupid. They're just thoughts. It's only natural to think them. Even in Centering Prayer we don't eliminate them. After a sit, one Catholic sister complained to Father Keating, "In twenty minutes I've had ten thousand thoughts!" Thomas famously replied, "How wonderful! Ten thousand opportunities to return to God."

Wrap your mind around that one.

Or don't. Just let it be.

Centering Prayer is a practice of failure. It's a fitness program for exercising surrender muscles. We learn strength in release, fortitude in despair, endurance in emptiness, generosity in repetition, devotion in effort. Silence in death. We consent, over and over, to love. In return, love shatters our smallness.

*

PERHAPS WHAT I sense in silence, what makes me long for it, is a power absolutely contrary to the domination dynamics of our world. It's like the difference between actively pumping oil from the desert then trucking it across the nation to burn, and building panels to receive the sun's energy. The first extracts, the second interacts. The first is willful, the second willing. Surrender, writes Cynthia Bourgeault, Episcopal priest and Centering Prayer guru, is not passive but rather the "active exercise of a receptive power." It's an alternative agency.

For decades I read the women mystics out of obligation (isn't this what a good contemplative woman does?) but couldn't handle their self-deprecation. Teresa of Avila was the worst. "I beg anyone who reads this account to bear in mind, for the love of the Lord, how wicked my life has been," she begins, and never lets up. Eventually I learned that Teresa's self-flagellation was likely a nod to the Inquisition, and suddenly saw her groveling as a veneer, not disingenuous but also not representing any core shame. Once you peel away the sin-talk, Teresa's cosmology is generous, generative, so unabashedly loving it turns our brokenness inside out and makes us shine. The irony of all those mystics (women and men) beating themselves up, calling themselves scummy sinners and advising us to surrender, is that such thinking never sent them to bed wallowing in self-hate. They became extraordinary writers and powerful leaders, people in no way hindered by a cosmology of humiliation: Teresa reforming the Carmelite order, Bonaventure heading the French academy and Franciscans, St. John of the Cross penning exquisite poetry while starving in jail, dame Julian counseling Norwich and beyond through the ravages of the plague… Their public lives were charged in a way that's puzzled me but now I understand. They didn't give up their agency; they just found a different fuel source.

In prayer, I observe my mind pumping out thoughts that go nowhere while real agency warms my cells until they bend toward the light. On the surface, surrender seems to undermine me while inside, my truest being swells.

*

I STUMBLE ONTO *The Way of the Pilgrim*, the story of a happy-go-lucky nineteenth century Russian mendicant's quest to pray without ceasing. He's a conversational guy, inquisitive, with not a cent in his pocket, a bum arm, restless feet, and a brain steeped in that text beloved in Eastern Orthodoxy for its pithy, practical wisdom, the *Philokalia*. He makes of himself a walking experiment for the Jesus Prayer. Three thousand repetitions a day. Out loud. For years. Until the prayer works its way into his system, his tongue moves without effort, and his heart pulses with the prayer's essence.

Out loud, the good pilgrim says.

You've got to be kidding, I say.

No; the words need to resonate in the diaphragm, vibrate in your blood. It's not enough to pray with head and heart. You need the body, too. This is biological transformation we're after, because without altering the configuration of our cells nothing else follows. Matter, energy—they're two states of the same substance. Ask any physicist. The container must open to the contents.

The winter walk to school works—I can hide my mouth behind a scarf—as does biking, with the roar of the wind and the privacy of speed, as does driving alone. I consider buying ear buds so I can pretend I'm on the phone. With each step I tumble down the staircase of humility. Only for twenty minutes, I reassure myself. Twenty minutes won't cause me to join the Moonies.

It's strange to engage in an activity that goes against your grain. Healthy eating is a good analogy. Always there's tension between the glazed doughnut that tastes great and the kale that tastes awful. But then the donut gives you a sugar crash, a belly ache, and love handles, while the kale gives you energy. Or consider exercise: The couch and a movie are gravitational while a workout requires a change of clothes, getting out of house, the distress of effort… I'm not of the mind that the doughnut is bad and kale is good; I like my doughnuts frosted, and an evening comatose in front of the TV is a respite from a busy week. I refuse to condemn this part of me as my sinful nature. At the same time I can't deny that this weak self, the small self, self-destructs. The less you eat doughnuts and the more you eat kale, the better kale tastes—and the more sickly sweet doughnuts become. The well-being that results from exercise is a reward couch-sitting will never match. The "grain" of our outsides quite naturally goes against the internal grain. The me who can't stomach a rote, antiquated, patriarchal prayer resides in the same person as the me who yearns for union. When I consent to caring for my body with kale and a bike ride,

I surrender my sugar-loving, lazy self to what is life-giving. During prayer, when I consent to God's presence and movement within me, I surrender self-righteousness and my distaste for religiosity and even my sense of having an independent identity to silence. I surrender to kenotic love, love that loves its way into my fullest self and then relinquishes that self into Love, which is a broader Self than I can imagine.

Biblical scholar Carroll Stuhlmueller called the psalms "a home lived in for many generations." I've moved into my ancestral home, the Jesus Prayer. Here's my renovation: *Divine One, who is both ultimate and particular, eternal and present, unfathomable and intimate, outside and in, worthy of worship and calling forth my best self: Whatever in me clings, relax. Whatever in me polarizes, connect. Whatever in me is hard, soften. Reunite me with the Whole.*

I use the rowing machine at the gym or pedal around Lake Nokomis or clean up after dinner and pray the traditional Jesus Prayer as best I can. Come to find out, this is Christian Yoga; it falls in a category of prayer transcending faith traditions called the Prayer of the Heart, which is why it causes my chest to fill and ache. On the landscape of my body this prayer carves a map to mercy. Christianity as I've come to understand it is a *practice*, a daily participation. What is strengthened within the scope of my heart muscles its way into my posture, my work, my relationships. I stay with the stretch; I hold it.

*

MEANWHILE, IN FRONT of my morning candle I can barely tolerate the parade of distractions—Emails! Pipelines! The pointlessness of meditation! Milk souring in the fridge!

Thoughts are my frantic effort to achieve union. Or internal scrambling to avoid it. Or a desperate attempt to matter. *Mercy,* a million *mercies.*

Gradually, over time, mercy metamorphosizes from diminishment to balm.

Sometimes I glimpse the consequences as I go about my days, always in my peripheral vision, never with certainty. When my lesson plan derails because everyone wants to read aloud their one-sentence memoirs—they're gasping and laughing and amazed by what they've done—I consent. My daughter can't sit still at the dinner table, and suddenly I see not her disrespect but her need for heavy muscle compression and I wheelbarrow her around the house. An oil company runs roughshod over native land, once again violating treaties, and I can't make it to the protest because I need to pick Gwyn up from school but I can call my legislators while she eats her snack. Emily and I play under the covers, her skin hot, her eyes soft, and an important deadline I've forgotten yanks my attention away, but then I notice; I release my sudden panic in favor of her lips, her neck, her sex. Even now, at my desk, suddenly my urgency to narrate prayer seems like self-indulgent naval-gazing, the memoirist's worst fear, but this is what presents itself so I concede. I don't know where God is in such moments. I don't often sense the silence. But there's enough life-energy pulsing here that, if I'm conscious, I can agree to it.

Consent isn't weak caving in, it's the opposite of compromising myself and a mightier thing altogether: An opening to love more powerful than I can fathom.

I want silence, I flee the silence, and silence is irrelevant—the point is practice. One does not release a thought in order to achieve some desired result (silence, rest, enlightenment). The releasing itself is the prayer's full meaning. *I consent to Your presence and movement.* I flex my surrender muscle. Spiritual body-building: the unmaking of strength as I know it. This is a regimen for imperceptible, reverse fitness.

*

THE GIFT OF having teachers is that occasionally they sound nonsensical but your respect for their intellect and your trust in their integrity recommend that you not dismiss them out of hand. Cynthia Bourgeault is my teacher. Mercy, she says, is the innermost quality of the Heart of God. Six years into my Centering Prayer practice I read her comment and scoff. How audacious is that?!

In Islam, Cynthia argues, mercy is the first of God's many names. Mercy is plastered across the Jewish scriptures, epitomized in Micah 6:8: "What does the Lord require of you? To act justly and to love mercy and to walk humbly with your God." The psalmist sings, "For as the heavens reach beyond earth and time, we swim in mercy as in an endless sea." While the word appears less frequently in the New Testament, Jesus's presence itself is an act of divine mercy and certainly his ministry pours mercy into broken lives.

Mercy, in short, is not what I've presumed. Its etymological seed is the ancient Etruscan word *merc*, from which sprung *commerce*, *merchant*, and the French *merci.* At its core, *mercy* describes connection and exchange. It is the stuff of relationship. The original Semitic, *chesed,* means "a fierce, bonding love." "*Chesed* is fidelity," Thomas Merton wrote. "It is ultimate and unfailing because it is the power that binds one person to another, in a covenant of hearts." Mercy is connective tissue. In both Hebrew and Arabic, the word *mercy* is the word for womb with different vowel points—our encompassing, nourishing origin.

I empty myself of all I've presumed about mercy to hear Bourgeault's definition: "Mercy is God's innermost being turned outward to sustain the visible and created world in unbreakable love."

> It is a substance. It actually exists. But it exists at a vibration so high, a frequency so intense, as to be barely contained within the created order; in fact, it often appears from our creaturely perspective to be a "nothing." It is the most intense and subtle energy that can exist within createdness. It is at the core of all things, the wellspring of being.

That singing silence from my dream! That field of unbounded rest! Life vibrating in my cells and the earth, binding microorganisms to soil to green sprouting plants to my mother's hands and my great-great-grandmother's heart to stardust, to fecund darkness. The dissolution of self into Self: Perhaps what I've sought from the start is mercy. The impulse seals me to my origins and end, a longing which is not me nor is it other than me.

Nothing's as it seems. I've swallowed the culture's typecast of mercy, hook, line, and sinker; I've denigrated it, colonized it, and only by exercising it do I meet it, at last, on its own terms. When mercy speaks for itself, I, too, am convinced mercy is love's DNA, irrevocably woven throughout creation's fabric.

"When I say, 'Lord have Mercy,' I am not making a pious devotional statement," Cynthia continues.

> It's not about worthy or unworthy, shame and guilt, blame and punishment. Rather, I am feeling to my very bones that yearning for being and sharing of being that permeates the entire created order. I am implicitly acknowledging that one cannot know without also *being known*. I am affirming my willingness to stay awake, to endure the vulnerability. I am actively engaging humility—not obsequiousness, but a recognition of the real scale of things, the depth of the suffering and the yearning that binds the created order to the uncreated light.

Mercy is the great womb of creation and

> does not come and go, granted to some and refused to others. Why? Because it is unconditional—always there, underlying everything. It is literally the force that holds everything in existence, the gravitational field in which "we live and move and have our being."

Whether or not this is true, whether or not a merciful heart is the energetic *being* of creation, I want it to be true and know my wanting and my acting help bring it about, at least in my small heart during prayer and at least in the lives of those I love, when, afterward, I turn my attention unequivocally toward them. Gwyn climbs into my lap. I receive her warmth, I offer my own.

Together we generate this reality.

*

THEN THERE'S THIS: I'm not supposed to consider my word at all. In Centering Prayer the sacred word is not a mantra, repeated until we've inhabited its every holy nuance. It's not a meditation—although this essay is. A sacred word is a reminder of our intent. It's a lasso of sounds meant to round up distractions.

I consent to releasing all that gets in the way of love's presence, which means thoughts, which means self, which means breath, which means *mercy*. If you meet the Buddha in the road, kill him. Or, as Thomas Keating quipped, if even the Virgin Mother Herself taps you on the shoulder while you're on your knees, say to her, "Not now, dearie. I'm doing my Centering Prayer."

*

AFTER EIGHT YEARS of practice, after four years of mapping mercy and thereby emptying the word of its charge, I was deep into a ten-day retreat when the rope by which I lowered myself into the well was cut. I floundered and splashed: terrifying, annihilating silence. Without thoughts I was all animal sensation—a frantically thumping chest, a buzzing in my groin, breathing so shallow I wondered if I'd survive. Who was I now? Aches in the knees, heat where the blanket wrapped my shoulders, the poignant arousal of spiritual longing, heavy sleepiness, the encroaching shiver and build-up of a sneeze. Eighteen hours of a nausea more energetic than physical. Vibrating silence. I'd never before been so alive.

Mercy vanished.

When I realized what had happened, I was elated. I'd touched down!

Later, the retreat director gravely informed me that, in the tradition of Centering Prayer, sensations are also "thoughts." As was my self-congratulations. I hadn't *arrived* anywhere because there's no place to arrive. Not only that: My *I* was false, and the touching down not of my own making. Then she sent me back to the cushion.

Now when *mercy* falls away my sacred word becomes the pressure of fifty-year-old knees on the floor. Every time I catch myself following the energy careening under my skin I return to that basic gravitational pull between body and earth. This too is mercy. The ground holds me whether or not I agree. The ground will hold me when I die. This is the peace of my cancer dream, my worst nightmare as well as my best hope. Emptiness is full. Spirit is matter. Death is really life.

*

IN THE DARK, secret center of ten silent days, my acts of consent are countless; I'm stripped of everything except my perpetual internal scrambling and that well-worn turn toward love when, finally, I see it: Even my consent isn't my own, even my longing. The part of me reaching into mystery isn't me. It's the bond in which I live and move and have my being: Mercy.

And the Jesus Prayer, whispered into my scarf under winter stars as I hike back and forth to the oratory—it's wiser than I am. Repeating it is how I confess I don't know what's right, what's good, even what prayer is. *You know. I only know in part; You know entirely.*

None of this matters—Centering Prayer, the Jesus Prayer, my endless ache, the vast, swallowing darkness, whatever I or anyone else posits of God. What matters is that I return home. I kiss my wife. I walk to school. In a gym stinky with kids, Gwyn spots me; she swishes over in her snowsuit and launches into my body for a pillowy collision, a reunion, this smallest of celebrations. Heading home, mittened hand in mittened hand, we are entirely here.

NOTES

Cynthia Bourgeault's words are taken from her books *Mystical Hope* and *The Holy Trinity and the Law of Three*, and from her commentaries on Gurdjieff's Lord Have Mercy exercise. Stories from Thomas Keating have been related orally within Contemplative Outreach, the organization he helped found. Wei Wu Wei's wisdom can be found in *Ask the Awakened*, Thomas Merton's in Thomas P. McDonnell's *The Merton Reader*, and Teresa of Avila's in her autobiography. All other teachings were related orally. More on Sharon Day's water ministry can be found at www.nibiwalk.org.

Much gratitude to Terrence Shaughnessy, whose steady listening embodies mercy.

ABOUT THE AUTHOR

Elizabeth Jarrett Andrew is the author of *Swinging on the Garden Gate: A Memoir of Bisexuality & Spirit*, now in its second edition; the novel *Hannah, Delivered*; a collection of personal essays, *On the Threshold: Home, Hardwood, and Holiness*; and three books on writing: *Writing the Sacred Journey: The Art and Practice of Spiritual Memoir*; *Living Revision: A Writer's Craft as Spiritual Practice*; and *The Release: Finding Creativity and Freedom After the Writing is Done*. She is a founding member of The Eye of the Heart Center, where she teaches writing as a transformational practice. She is a recipient of two Minnesota State Arts Board artists' fellowships, The Loft Career Initiative Grant, and is a Minnesota Book Awards finalist.

ABOUT ORISON BOOKS

Orison Books is a 501(c)3 non-profit literary press focused on the life of the spirit from a broad and inclusive range of perspectives. We seek to publish books of exceptional poetry, fiction, and non-fiction from perspectives spanning the spectrum of spiritual and religious thought, ethnicity, gender identity, and sexual orientation.

As a non-profit literary press, Orison Books depends on the support of donors. To find out more about our mission and our books, or to make a donation, please visit www.orisonbooks.com.

Orison Books is deeply grateful to our recurring annual donors for sustaining our important work. If you'd like to make a recurring or one-time contribution, please visit www.orisonbooks.com/support-us.

Sustainers' Circle

Carol Dines
Michele Laub
Laura & Barry Rand
Bruce Spang
Lee Stockdale
Anonymous

Advocates' Circle

David Ebenbach
Anonymous

Supporters' Circle

Nickole Brown
Richard Chess

Friends' Circle

Paige Gilchrist
Laurel Haavik
Alida Woods

www.ingramcontent.com/pod-product-compliance
Lightning Source LLC
Chambersburg PA
CBHW021724190726
48289CB00008B/2686

* 9 7 8 1 9 4 9 0 3 9 6 6 5 *